SCHOLASTIC discover more™

Farm

By Penelope Arlon
and Tory Gordon-Harris

How to discover more

Farm is specially planned to help you discover more about farm life and animals on every page.

Big words and pictures introduce an important subject.

Picture sequences show what happens in detail.

Small words help you explore pictures for active reading.

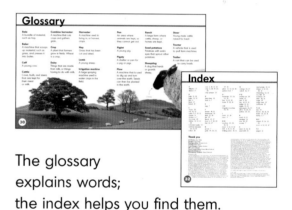

The glossary explains words; the index helps you find them.

Digital companion book

Download your free all-new digital book, **Farm Fun!**

Log on to
**www.scholastic.com/
discovermore**

Enter your unique code:
RMHJC6HCG2X7

Fun farm activities

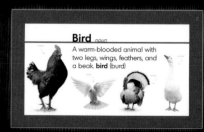

More farm words

Contents

Literacy Consultant: Barbara Russ, 21st Century Community Learning Center Director for Winooski (Vermont) School District

Library of Congress Cataloging-in-Publication Data Available

ISBN 978-0-545-36571-0

10 9 8 7 6 5 4 3 2 1   12 13 14 15 16

Printed in Singapore   46
First edition, January 2012

The farm

Farms are large areas of land for growing plants or keeping animals.

Crop farms

Farm plants are called crops. Most crops are grown for food.

corn

Animal farms

Animals are kept on farms for food and for materials, such as wool.

sheep give wool

Farms are very important because they produce most of the food we eat.

Farms produce food.

Food is sent to grocery stores.

We buy the food to eat.

Some cows are kept for meat. Others are kept for their milk.

dairy cow

5

Farm birds

Farm birds can often be seen in farmyards or in farm ponds.

Turkeys make funny gobbling sounds.

Chickens are the most popular farm birds.

Ducks like to swim in farm ponds and streams.

6

A mother chicken, called a hen, can lay eggs for your breakfast.

A duck's foot is webbed for paddling through water.

A hen has claws for running on hard ground.

duck

turkey

goose

rooster

guinea fowl

Cattle ranch

In the United States, cattle are kept on huge farms called ranches.

Grazing cattle

The cattle graze, or feed on, open areas and can move around wherever they like.

Moving on

A herder herds, or gathers, them on horseback when he wants to take them to a new area to feed.

These people are cattle herders. They are known as cowboys.

Catching cattle

If an animal escapes, the herders sometimes use a special rope, called a lasso, to catch it.

In the pen

When the cattle are ready to be taken to the market to be sold, they are herded into a pen.

Dairy farm

Some farms keep cows for their milk. These farms are called dairy farms.

A cow must have a calf before it can make milk.

silo

Farmers often live near their animals so they can look after them.

barn

farmhouse

milking parlor

Cows eat grass in the summer and hay in the winter.

Cows are milked in a milking parlor, often twice a day.

Milk can be made into many different cheeses and yogurts.

Milk is good for us.
It keeps our bones strong.

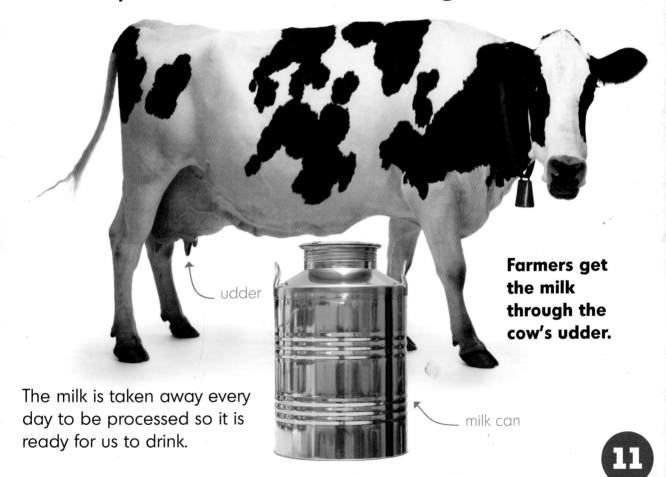

udder

milk can

Farmers get the milk through the cow's udder.

The milk is taken away every day to be processed so it is ready for us to drink.

Woolly sheep

Sheep have woolly coats. We knit the wool to make clothes.

In the spring, sheep give birth to lambs. They often have twins.

Sheep eat grass. They like to stay close to one another when they graze the grass.

12

A sheep's coat is called a fleece.

Sheep live outside all year. Their woolly fleeces keep them warm.

Farmers sometimes use sheepdogs to herd sheep together.

In early summer, the sheep are brought in to be sheared, or shaved.

The sheared fleece is turned into wool for our clothes.

sheepdog

wool

Pig farm

Pigs love to wallow in mud in the hot summer months. They do this to keep cool.

piglet

Pigs live in big fields on farms. They are kept for their meat.

Farmers feed the pigs pellets, which are made of a mix of foods to keep them healthy.

mother pig

Mother pigs can have as many as sixteen piglets at one time.

Some pigs are kept outside in big fields. They sleep in little shelters called pigsties.

You may think all pigs are pink, but some are black or brown, and some have spots!

15

Rare farms

There are some very unusual farm animals in the world.

reindeer

Reindeer are herded in some Arctic areas. The herders live in tents and move with the reindeer.

Ostriches are farmed around the world. Their feathers are used for feather dusters!

alligator

alpaca

bison

Some people farm alligators. They must be very brave!

Alpacas are farmed for their thick, woolly fleeces. The fleeces are knitted into clothes.

American bison are sometimes raised for their meat.

ostrich

Crops

Crops are plants that farmers grow in big fields. Most crops are grown for food.

After the farmer has cut the crops, they are stored in large buildings before being sent to the market.

grain stores

grain elevator

Here are some common crops.

wheat grain

Seeds from the wheat plant are ground into flour, which is used to make bread.

soybeans

Soybeans can be crushed to make soy milk.

sunflower seeds

The seeds from sunflowers are used to make cooking oil.

sugar beets

Some sugar comes from the root of the sugar beet plant.

Tractors

Tractors drive slowly and pull machines that do all kinds of work around the farm.

For thousands of years, animals were used to pull farm machinery. Horses did much of the heavy work that modern tractors do today.

A plow digs up the earth. Then seeds can be planted.

A baler scoops up cut grass and presses it into hay bales.

A trailer helps the farmer carry loads around the farm.

Farm machines

These machines are used to farm potatoes. Farms use many machines.

Plow

plow

A plow digs trenches so seed potatoes—used to grow other potatoes—can fall deep into the soil.

Seed drill

A seed drill is a machine that drops the seed potatoes into the ground.

Irrigation machine

young potato plant

The potato plants are watered regularly using an irrigation machine.

Crop sprayer

Crops are sometimes sprayed with chemicals to get rid of pests. The Colorado beetle eats potato crops.

crop sprayer

Colorado beetle

Harvester

truck

tractor with harvester

When the potatoes are ready, a harvester digs them up and tips them into a truck.

Sorter

The potatoes are sorted by hand to remove any bad ones.

flowering potato plant

Harvesting

When wheat needs to be cut, a combine harvester begins its work.

wheat grain

combine harvester

grain spout

wheat grain

cutting blades

24

Cutting the crop

Combine harvesters cut the wheat and gather the grain.

The grain is taken away in a trailer.

The leftover wheat stems are turned into straw.

Look out for mice—they like wheat, too!

Fruit farms

The fruit we buy in stores is grown on farms, big and small, in many different countries.

There are many orange farms in California and Florida. They are called groves.

orange grove

Some fruits, such as oranges and pineapples, grow in hot places.

orange

A machine waters the orange plants by spraying them.

When the oranges are ripe, they are often picked by hand.

People check the oranges before they are sold.

Many types of fruit are soft, so they have to be picked carefully.

water tower

pineapple

strawberry

raspberry

apple

Some fruits, such as berries and apples, grow in cool places.

Other farms

Farms around the world produce many different foods and materials.

Rice that has not been processed is known as paddy rice or rough rice.

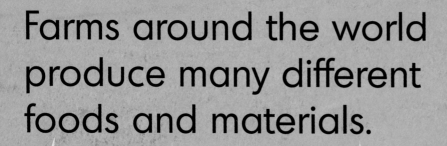

Chocolate

Chocolate comes from the seeds of the cacao tree.

Cotton

The cotton that we use to make clothes grows on shrubs.

Rice farming

In many parts of the world, rice grains are picked by hand.

Fish

Fish are sometimes farmed in big lakes or along an ocean's coast.

Tea

Tea leaves grow in huge fields in warm climates.

Glossary

Bale
A bundle of material, such as hay.

Baler
A machine that scoops up material, such as grass, and presses it into bales.

Calf
A young cow.

Cattle
Cows, bulls, and steers that are kept for their meat or milk.

Combine harvester
A machine that cuts crops and gathers grain.

Crop
A plant that farmers grow in fields. Wheat is a crop.

Dairy
Things that are made from milk, or things having to do with milk.

Harvester
A machine used to bring in, or harvest, crops.

Hay
Grass that has been cut and dried.

Irrigation machine
A large spraying machine used to water crops in the field.

Lamb
A young sheep.

Pen
An area where animals are kept, so they cannot get out.

Piglet
A young pig.

Pigsty
A shelter or pen for a pig or pigs.

Plow
A machine that is used to dig up and turn over the earth. Seeds can then be planted in the earth.

Ranch
A large farm where cattle, sheep, or horses are kept.

Seed potatoes
Potatoes with extra eyes that sprout other potatoes.

Sheepdog
A dog that herds or guards sheep.

Steer
Young male cattle raised for beef.

Tractor
A vehicle that is used to pull farm machines.

Trailer
A cart that can be used to carry loads.

sheep

Index

Thank you

Art Director: Bryn Walls
Designer: Ali Scrivens
Managing Editor: Miranda Smith
US Editor: Beth Sutinis
Cover Designer: Natalie Godwin
DTP: John Goldsmid
Visual Content Editor: Diane Allford-Trotman
Executive Director of Photography, Scholastic: Steve Diamond

Photography credits
1: PhotoHouse/Shutterstock; 3: Tim Scrivener/Alamy; 4tl: Paul-André Belle-Isle/Shutterstock; 4tr: Jeffrey Van Daele/Shutterstock; 4m: Kateryna Dyellalova/Shutterstock; 4–5 (front): Morgan DDL/Shutterstock; 4–5 (back): otonio/iStockphoto; 5tl: Matthew Jacques/Shutterstock; 5tc: Baevskiy Dmitry/Shutterstock; 5tr: Paul Cowan/Shutterstock; 5b: Worldpics/Shutterstock; 6tl: David Chapman/Alamy; 6ml: Walter Quirtmair/Alamy; 6bl: Maximilian Weinzierl/Alamy; 6–7 (front): Carolinasmith/Dreamstime.com; 6–7 (back): Andynwt/iStockphoto; 7tl: Neil Setchfield/Alamy; 7tr: National Geographic Image Collection/Alamy; 7bl: u-Lee/iStockphoto; 7bcl: Chepko/iStockphoto; 7bc: Gary Ombler/Scholastic; 7bcr: NatalyaAksenova/iStockphoto; 7br: GlobalP/iStockphoto; 8bl: Mike Boyatt/AgStock Images/Corbis; 8br: James L. Amos/Corbis; 8–9t: Nicolas Russell/Getty Images; 9tr: debibishop/iStockphoto; 9bl: David Stoecklein/Corbis; 9br: Sasha Woolley/Corbis; 10: Matthew Jacques/Shutterstock; 10tr: 10274693/iStockphoto; 11tl: Stock Connection Blue/Alamy; 11tc: Agripicture Images/Alamy; 11tr: Shebeko/Shutterstock; 11m: Ocean/Corbis; 11b: imagestock/iStockphoto; 12tr: Eric Isselée/Shutterstock; 12b: Trevor Kelly/Shutterstock; 12–13 (back): CaptureLight/Shutterstock; 13tl: CaptureLight/Shutterstock; 13mla: Wayne Hutchinson/AgStock Images/Corbis; 13mlb: Pichugin Dmitry/Shutterstock; 13bl: esemelwe/iStockphoto; 13tr: Eric Isselée/Shutterstock; 13br: esemelwe/iStockphoto; 14: PhotoHouse/Shutterstock; 15tl: Anat-oli/Shutterstock; 15tr: Carmen Jaspersen/dpa/Corbis; 15m: oneo/Shutterstock; 15bl: Matthew Mawson/Alamy; 15br: Tim Graham/Alamy; 16tr: Eric Isselée/Shutterstock; 16–17 (front): nadi555/Shutterstock; 16–17 (back): Kypros/Alamy; 17tl: fivespots/Shutterstock; 17tc, 17tr: Eric Isselée/Shutterstock; 18–19: jameslee999/iStockphoto; 19tl: Zeljko Radojko/Shutterstock; 19tc: Tomo Jesenicnik/Shutterstock; 19tr: photolino/Shutterstock; 19mla: Kimberly Hall/Shutterstock; 19mca: Tomo Jesenicnik/Shutterstock; 19mra: JCREATION/Shutterstock; 19mlb: Pakhnyushcha/Shutterstock; 19mcb: Living Food/Shutterstock; 19mrb: Kotkin Vasily/Shutterstock; 19bl: Robert Biedermann/Shutterstock; 19bc: Luis Carlos Jimenez del rio/Shutterstock; 19br: Juris Sturainis/Shutterstock; 20bl: Mary Evans Picture Library/Alamy; 20–21: AgStock Images/Corbis; 21tl: Tim Scrivener/Alamy; 21tc: DanDriedger/iStockphoto; 21tr: mbtaichi/iStockphoto; 22tl: Orientaly/Shutterstock; 22tr: Jakub Pavlinec/Shutterstock; 22mr: Rafai Fabrykiewicz/Shutterstock; 22bl: Vasllius/Shutterstock; 22–23b: GeorgeClerk/iStockphoto; 23tl: Mountainpix/Shutterstock; 23tr: Ivaschenko Roman/Shutterstock; 23mla: Denton Rumsey/Shutterstock; 23mlb: Lasse Kristensen/Shutterstock; 23mr: Ridofranz/iStockphoto; 23br: Sergii Figurnyi/Shutterstock; 24: Ian Sanderson/Getty Images; 24tr: J.Hall/photocuisine/Corbis; 25l: imagewerks/Getty Images; 25tr: Cornstock/Getty Images; 25mra: Dave Reede/Getty Images; 25mrb: David R. Frazier Photolibrary, Inc./Alamy; 25br: Oxford Scientific/Getty Images; 26bl: William Manning/Alamy; 26–27a: Richard Thornton/Shutterstock; 26–27b: ValentynVolkov/iStockphoto; 27tl: David Thurber/AgStock Images/Corbis; 27tc: Rolf Richardson/Alamy; 27tr: David Thurber/AgStock Images/Corbis; 27bl: Viktar Malyshchyts/Shutterstock; 27bcl: topshotUK/iStockphoto; 27bcr: roman_sh/iStockphoto; 27br: Gary Ombler/Scholastic; 28ml: Greenshoots Communications; 28 bl: Antonio V. Oquias/Shutterstock; 28mr: GONUL KOKAL/Shutterstock; 28br: mexrix/Shutterstock; 28–29 (back): David Berry/Shutterstock; 28–29 (front): zhuda/Shutterstock; 29ml: Kang Khoon Seang/Shutterstock; 29bl: Krasowit/Shutterstock; 29mr: Eky Studio/Shutterstock; 29br: Viktor1/Shutterstock; 30–31 (back): CaptureLight/Shutterstock; 31br: Eric Isselée/Shutterstock.

The credits for the images on page 2 can be found on pages 12–13 and 30–31.

Cover credits
Front tl: Digital Vision/Getty Images; tc: Digital Vision/Getty Images; tr: Siede Preis/Getty Images; b (back): Wolfgang Kaehler/Corbis; b (front): Serhii Novikov/Fotolia. Back tl: Tamara Staples/Getty Images; tc: Fuse/Getty Images; tr: Gordon Clayton/Getty Images; bl: Manaemedia | Dreamstime.com.